HAND IN HAND

Laura Margaret Evans

HAND IN HAND

MOTHER, CHILD AND GOD

FLEMING H. REVELL COMPANY

To my mother
for the exquisite pattern
of her love

AND

To my daughters
Pamela, Paula, and Linda
whose hands in mine have made me
ever aware of my need to reach out daily
for the hand of God

Introduction

IT WAS IN late November, 1953, that I first became aware of Laura Margaret Evans. That fall I was in Hollywood for a series of script conferences on *A Man Called Peter*. By pre-arrangement, Laura Margaret's mother and I met for lunch at the studio commissary on the 20th Century-Fox lot. Neither of us was much interested that day in celebrity-watching. Motion picture personalities whose names were household words came and went. We didn't notice; more important matters occupied us.

Mrs. Evans brought bad news. Laurie was seriously ill. A chain of prayer for her was going on day and night at the Hollywood Presbyterian Church.

"You've been through some rough waters yourself," Mrs. Evans said. "In *A Man Called Peter* you wrote of how a prayer of relinquishment concerning your own health was wonderfully answered. I'm here to find out exactly what you mean by 'a prayer of relinquishment.' Tell me all you know—"

7

The eyes across the table looked straight into mine. Our lunch lasted a long time. . . . I shared all that I could out of my limited knowledge of that gigantic subject—prayer. Prayer—still, even in our day—is largely unexplored terrain.

Finally Mrs. Evans and I parted, she to go back to her vigil in the hospital, I to walk back to the movie producer's office. The California sunshine was warm on my face. I scarcely felt it.

A year passed. From time to time I heard news of Laurie, recovered and back with her family. Then in the summer of 1959 there came to my desk the manuscript of *Hand in Hand*. I had not read ten pages before I knew that here was one specific answer to all the prayers that had gone up for Laura Margaret Evans.

Hand in Hand is part of the answer. How can I be sure? Because in these pages is as sensitive a spirit as I have ever met. Here is one who cherishes every moment on this lovely earth. Here is awareness born of being a wife and mother.

It is an awareness of small joys—she speaks of "the patio flooded with silver"; "the silhouettes of the leaves like delicate black lace"; "bright flowers and tangy water cress beside the brook"; "blueberry muffins"; and "bushy-tailed squirrels." It is an awareness too of more important things—like provocative questions and shy dreams in the hearts of little girls.

INTRODUCTION

Hand in Hand will inevitably be a part of the future that a loving God has planned for Laura Margaret Evans. Through these pages I glimpse the shining through of another Spirit beyond the author's own. Here, other mothers will find a new awareness too. They will find some answers that the books on child psychology ignore. With joy I commend to you this sharing from the deeps of a mother's heart.

CATHERINE MARSHALL

Washington, D. C.

9

Contents

CONTENTS

HAND IN HAND

I Don't Want To Go to Heaven

"I don't want to go to heaven!"

The little face beside mine is almost rebellious. I know how she feels. Being outdoors on a day like today, when the rich brown loam is an intoxicating fragrance, when the grass is warm and sweet, when the birds are friendly and brave, makes God's lovely, lovely earth a place so beautiful it brings an ache to the soul.

Yes, I know how she feels. How could anything be this perfect? I break a damp clod of earth between my fingers and watch as the soil crumbles around the newly planted seedling. A delicate brown spider scurries past in haste and a silver-gray sowbug lumbers into a crevice.

"I think heaven will be awful, Mommy. Everything

gold and ivory and things. It will be too shiny and hurt my eyes."

She lies full length on the grass, her lean body pressed against its lush softness, drinking up its sweet goodness. "I like the grass and the smell and I love my little brown towhee. My brown towhee couldn't live in heaven because there won't be trees."

"Darling, who do you think planned this earth?"

"God did. Everybody knows that."

"Do you like the way He made things?"

"Yes. I think it's just perfect."

"And we're not even supposed to live here forever, are we?"

"No, but I wish we could. I don't want to die and leave it."

"Of course you don't yet. You've hardly gotten to know it. You're still exploring and discovering new things. And you always will, if you try. But the truth is, we are not meant to stay here forever. God has a better place fixed for us."

"Well, I don't think it could be better. The Bible says the streets are paved with gold. They'll be hot. I like trails and paths like at the lake."

"Don't you think that if God could make a place like this that we love so much, that He could do even better in a place where we are going to live forever?"

"I don't know. I don't know if I want to live forever."

16

"But don't you think if we are going to live forever, that heaven will be even more beautiful than what we know now?"

"But we already know what heaven's going to be like and I don't want to go."

"St. Paul says, 'Eye hath not seen, nor ear heard, neither have entered into the heart of man, the things which God hath prepared for them that love him.' So no one knows. We cannot even imagine how wonderful it's going to be."

"But the man who wrote Revelation says it's going to be gold and things."

"But he was talking about God's Holy City, not all of heaven. Even our cities here are not the same as our lakes and country, are they?"

"No, I guess not. But will there be trees and roses and towhees and things I like, Mommy?"

"If heaven is a place where we are completely content and happy, then everything we will need or want will be there. We may desire different things. We may have different ideas of what can make us happy there."

"Well, maybe. But it scares me to think of going there."

"Anything new or unknown has a way of making all of us afraid a little. But the main thing for us to learn here in this earth is this one big thing: how much God loves us. Once you begin to understand even the tiniest bit how very, very great His love is for us, you will never be afraid of anything He plans for you. Because

17

you trust Him enough, you will know that He only plans the best for us. Don't worry. Just try to know Him better and better, and one of these days, nothing can make you really afraid."

"Does He love me as much as you do, Mommy?"

"Even more, baby."

The little face is still now and the mouth is soft and curved. "Then I guess I won't be afraid any more."

I'll Be Your Friend

"I hate school!"

"Why, dear? What on earth happened?"

"The kids are so mean! I never want to see them again!"

"What did they do?"

"They teased Belle and teased her and teased her. I could just hit them all!"

"Who is Belle?"

"She's the new girl with the straight hair and funny clothes."

"Well, surely they didn't pick on her for that?"

"I don't know why they did, but they did. She does talk kind of funny, Mother."

"How did you treat her?" (The blue eyes slid away from mine. She didn't answer for a moment.)

"Well, they made me do it! They wouldn't let her in the rope game and I was ahead. I couldn't just *leave*, Mother!"

"Did you speak to her at all?"

"No. I just got mad at the kids."

"Did anyone make friends with her?"

"No."

"She must be pretty lonely right now."

"She probably won't come back to that dumb old school."

"Oh, she'll come back. She has to. But she probably won't want to. You have a lot of friends, don't you, dear?"

(She looked at me warily.) "Yes, I guess so."

"You would be pretty unhappy without any, wouldn't you?"

"Yes."

"Are you afraid to be nice to Belle? Are you afraid the other girls would hurt you?"

"No, they wouldn't hurt me." (She looked at me for a moment. Then she shrugged.) "I guess they'd just think I was crazy or something."

"Are you afraid of them laughing at you?"

"I don't know."

"Are you afraid they wouldn't play with you, either?"

"I guess so."

"Well, you won't really know until you have tried, will you?"

20

"No."

"Why don't you try sitting beside her at lunch. That's always a good time to get to know someone. You never can tell—you might find out she's fun. Sometimes the nice things we do for others turn out to be even nicer for us. Did you know that?"

"No. Well, all right, I'll try. But I don't think it will work."

"Mother, it did work!"

"Belle?"

"Yes. And you know something? She lived in France for a while and she's teaching me French words. We talked some French words and the other girls wanted to know what we were talking."

"Did they want to play with her?"

"No, not yet. But Chris gave her a piece of fudge and Donna helped her pick up her papers when they spilled. I don't think they like her, though."

"They probably will in time. Did they laugh at you?"

"No. They just looked at me kind of funny when I sat down beside her."

"What did Belle say?"

"Nothing at first. She just looked up when I came over and then when I sat beside her, she smiled. We didn't talk very much. But she gave me some real neat cookies. Her mother had sent some to school to give the kids but I don't think she knew how to give them out. I told her to save some for tomorrow and there would probably be lots of girls who would want some. They had peach stuffing inside. Mother, would you feel bad if people weren't nice to me?"

"Oh yes, darling. I don't think anything can hurt a mother quite as much as having her child hurt or laughed at."

"I guess that's why Belle's mother made the cookies for her. She wanted to help her make friends. I'm glad I sat beside her today."

I could only nod, for the lump in my throat. . . .

What Shall I Be?

"What are you filling out?"

"Just a form. We're supposed to put down what we want to be when we grow up. For college credits."

"Oh. Do you know what you want to be?"

"Yes, but everyone will think I'm a 'square.'"

"Why?"

"Well, there's not much money in the first one and *no one* wants to be the second."

"Could I ask what they are?"

"Yes. You'll understand because they'd think you're a 'square,' too, Mother!" She looked at me and we both laughed. "First, I would like to write and illustrate books for children—really good books, Mother. Books that help them pretend they can be someone good and wonderful.

The kind of book that makes them think of beautiful things. Then, most of all I want to be married to someone I love very much. I want to have children and live on a ranch as close to the Tetons as I can get."

She looked at me with complete confidence in my approval. I had to smile. "And they would think that's being 'square'?"

She nodded. Then she looked away, out of the windows toward our canyon that was now already brushed golden with autumn. There was a sudden wistfulness in her eyes and her voice was soft and a little tight when she spoke. "Mother, do you suppose there will be a boy somewhere, who will feel like I do? Who will like the things I like and won't be afraid of what the other fellows think? Do you think there will be someone who won't think I'm stupid and who will understand about my books?"

"I know there will be. And perhaps he's wondering right now if he will ever find a girl like you . . . a girl who understands love and dreams and who wouldn't think he was wrong because he wanted to be a rancher or a chemist or a teacher or anything else . . . a girl who could give him a home and children. Somewhere, he's wondering if he'll ever find you."

. . . and somewhere, there is a mother who is reassuring him, with her heart in her throat, saying "Please, dear God, let it be true. . . ."

God Is Not Like That

Mrs. B—— has just left, and her words are still filling the room: "I simply won't accept the fact that you are not going to be healed! God does not expect any of us to be sick. You must have more faith, my dear."

Why can I sit here and smile at those words now? They used to fill me with frustration and bewilderment and anger—and guilt for such obvious lack of faith on my part. She means well, but how can I make her understand? How can I tell her what my faith is? How can I show her that my faith is grown, now? It is no longer unembodied stuff, without form or definition. My faith is as high as heaven and as sufficient as God Himself.

She won't accept the fact? I have. Well-meaning friends said it was resignation; well, perhaps it was for a time. There comes the moment when we fight no more, we lie limp and empty. But resignation is death and barren; nothing springs from it. It is bitterness with a sophisticated hat, trying to look presentable. Someone told me it was fatalism, but fatalism is without reason and demands no responsibility. It is living in a rowboat without oars. Mine is acceptance. Just that, nothing more. It has opened the door of freedom for me. I am accepting it one day at a time. For now. Until the next step. Acceptance is the waiting room of Hope. I do not even hope yet. I am just waiting and listening.

And how can she—or I—know what God expects? Who am I to step into His throne room and demand an explanation for His actions? Sergeants at war have more respect than this. And this is war, this life. I am scarcely a soldier yet. Still, am I supposed to know what God expects? No, I think not.

All I do know at this moment is that I have committed my life to Him. Either He is great enough to know what He is about and strong enough to carry it through if I remain committed and pliable and do not hamper His plan . . . or else He is uncertain, easily swayed, a God to be coaxed and moved according to the whining of an undisciplined child. I do not permit my children to whine and coax. Once they ask, I know they desire. They must trust my judgment, put their faith in my love for them.

26

And so must I toward God. The only faith I need now is faith in His perfect plan for me, faith that His love for me is more eternal than my life, and that His judgment runs ahead of me, far into the future.

This is God's war. I have enlisted to serve and follow His orders. I doubt that He will ask me in to view His map; I do not think He will ask my opinion on this enormous battle that is being waged. Were I to disobey His command, or were I to run to the other camp . . . then yes, I think He would call for me and I should not want to look at Him. I have cast my lot. I shall trust and do the thing that is given me.

It's true, when I said I wanted to enlist, I had other things in mind, things which came easily to me and which I could do well. Somehow, I feel awkward and out of place here, but there is a reason. I may never know. Or perhaps I shall. It doesn't matter.

I Don't Ever Want To Marry!

The night is so clear and dark, and yet not all dark. It seems the stars are giving a silver sharpness to things. I can almost see the soft roundness of her cheek as she sleeps now. Such a troubled day. She is starting to grow up. The bud is unfurling a little and as the flower opens, it is so vulnerable. I have prayed all week that the words I would offer would be the right ones. That they would open these strange doors into wonder and mystery, not into horror and distaste.

All this month I have seen this troubled, unspoken question in her eyes, as she weighs this thought against that, holding herself aloof a little, afraid of the truth, yet more afraid to be left out. I think perhaps all is well, though; and thank you, God, for the words, and for

28

having sanctified long ago this act of love through marriage. Please let it always be a thing of wonder and sweetness and specialness for her.

I knew this would be a difficult day since we talked yesterday. I knew the questions would start and have dark shadows stalking them. I tried to be young again and feel as I know she felt. I tried to remember the things in which I needed reassurance. How well I understood that explosive indignation of her young innocence as it tried to condone such adult acceptance of something so strange and frightening. I remember the loathing. The disbelief. The angry hurt, the withdrawing.

I think she is beginning now to understand a little, the difference—the only two things which can make the difference—sanctification on Your part, Lord, and pure, complete love on her part. Without these, truly the act is one to loathe.

She had said, "But Mother! It's so awful. It's everything that's bad. Why does it have to be that way? Why!"

"Because this is the way God meant it to be. And whatever God plans is good and right. It's only when things are out of place or misused that they become disgusting or evil. You love the smell of fresh earth after Dad has spaded, don't you?"

"Yes."

"It is soil and it is good and rich and has a very special something that enables things to grow. It is wonderful and mysterious and we accept it for its worth. But when we bring this same soil into our home, it becomes plain dirt. It makes things messy and unattractive and we get rid of it as soon as we can. It's the same substance, but out of place."

She was silent, still resisting this new thing.

"Darling, marriage was created for us, first of all, to keep us from being lonely, to make sure that we would have someone whom we loved with all our hearts and who would love us in return; and secondly, in order to 'replenish the earth,' by giving other little lives a chance to live and know God and become part of His world. And it is only when this is used for selfish or harmful purposes that it becomes anything else."

"But I don't think I could ever love anyone *that* much! No one!"

"You're still not yet grown up so of course you don't understand. You are not ready to, yet, but some day you will and you will remember what we have said today about keeping things in their right place so that they stay beautiful and fresh. When you love someone enough, you don't mind sharing yourself with them. You share things with me that you wouldn't with a stranger, don't you?"

"Yes, but you're my mother."

"When you fall in love with a fine man, you will feel

as close to him—even closer. And that is why it's so important that he be a Christian and know and respect God as you do. Otherwise, things that are sacred to you won't be to him and he might laugh at your ideals. If you both love God and desire to keep this thing beautiful and special, it won't be hard. But if he does not know God as you do, then even after you are married you can never really share your friendship, your dreams, your feeling for the big things. You'll always feel a little alone and a little hungry for someone to understand and share your soul with you."

"How do you know when you're really in love like that?"

"As you grow older, you'll be able to tell better and better. There will be times, too, when you may think you are really in love and you will have to wait and see. But that's a bridge we cross when we come to it."

She had smiled a little then. "Well, I guess if you felt the same way and got over it, I can too. But it will take a while."

"Of course, it will. But just remember the two important things—God has blessed marriage and when you love someone very deeply, marriage can be the finest thing in the world. . . ."

And as she sleeps now, please place Thy seal upon her heart. Make these things lovely and right and lift the heaviness from her heart. Let her knowledge free her from the guilty whispers in the school lavatory and from the nasty jokes on the playground. Help her hold her secret apart and clean, and please, God, let there be a boy somewhere who will one day make this hope a reality and this trust an answered prayer, and this dream come true.   Amen.

To Die and Grow Again

"My Sunday school teacher said we'll have new bodies in heaven. I don't want a new body. I like mine. If I have a new one, no one will know me."

"Jesus said we will know each other, though. He showed us that when He appeared to His disciples after His death. Don't you remember?"

"Yes, but they didn't know Him at first."

"Not until He did something. What was it?"

"Well, He broke the bread and then they knew it was Jesus."

"We may still have the same mannerisms and ways of doing things. It may be that that will distinguish us."

"But how can we get a new body if our real one goes

into dust. You know, Mommy, even bones go away after lots of years."

"Do you remember the seed the teacher gave you to plant when you came home a few weeks ago from Sunday school?"

"Yes. It wasn't a seed, though, it was a bean."

"That is the seed of the bean plant."

"Oh. Well, it grew into a bean plant. It's not very big, though."

"What happened to the seed?"

"Well, first it broke when the leaves came out and then I couldn't find it after a while when the stem was big."

"But the seed had to die before the beautiful plant could grow, didn't it?"

"Yes."

"Which do you think is more beautiful—the brown seed you planted or the plant that is growing?"

"The plant, of course, Mommy."

"I think perhaps we will be just that much more beautiful in heaven than we are here, too."

"Will I have leaves?"

"No, you won't have leaves. You're a person, not a plant. We don't plant marigold seeds and get carrots or puppies, do we?"

She laughed. "No. But Mommy, if people put us in boxes and the dirt doesn't touch us, how can we grow? I mean when we're buried, we can't grow roots."

34

"God is just trying to show us that life continues even after there seems to be death. It doesn't mean that everything happens exactly the same. But He is trying to explain the principle of Life to us in everything that grows."

"What is 'principle' of life?"

"The principle of something is the important part of it. Like the important thing we learn from planting a seed is that, even though the seed dies, the living part of it doesn't die if it's healthy and well cared for. Our souls are like the living part of our seed. Our body, our outer seed-part can die, but if we've kept our soul healthy, then it will be released and go on living."

"When I look at a seed, it doesn't look like it could have such a beautiful plant inside it. I wonder if I will be beautiful in heaven."

"I'm sure you will. God says all our bodies will be glorified. That means they are going to be something pretty special."

"But Mommy!" There was sudden fear in her eyes. "What of the people who get burned or get drowned to death?"

"People are different from seeds in this way, dear. No matter what happens to the body before or after death, the soul is still free. You see, plants were meant to grow again on this earth. But we were meant to grow again in heaven, so what happens before or after we die here isn't important."

"Oh. Well, I'm glad I'm not old yet. I think I'll be a seed a little longer before I'm a germ of my seed. I'm going down to swing now, Mommy. I love you."

God Has Sent You

Some mornings I feel as though I could tackle anything that might come. Today is one of those days. I feel strong and quiet and full of deep reserves. I do not think even the phone ringing or a peddler at the door could disturb me this morning.

Even this little admonition I have just read does not seem unreasonable. . . . "Take everything as it comes; accept it with willingness, yea, with cheerfulness. It is sent of God. Receive it and your heart shall be regenerated and restored."

Is that one of the secrets of those early Quaker women? The secret of their constant poise and lack of irritation? The practice that made them eager and interested and capable and stimulating?

It is so hard for me to put aside something I am right in the midst of doing! I even dislike having to interrupt my housework for a phone call. I resent seeing salesmen when my ironing is waiting. I even resist the requests of my friends and family when I am not prepared to give extra time. Being an organized person sometimes makes me quick and aloof. I must watch that.

". . . accept with willingness . . . cheerfulness. It is sent of God." Forgive me for yesterday, then! Liz called and wanted me to come over. She did sound so discouraged and blue, and I said, "Maybe some other day. I'm swamped." I might have been able to help by just listening. As it was, the day was gone anyway, because I got involved in cupboards and didn't have enough storage boxes to finish. It serves me right . . . if I had gone to Liz. . . .

And the funny little fruit man. He was so tired. I knew he must be thirsty and I should have offered him a cold drink but he was such a talker and my cupboards were waiting!

I wonder how much I miss by shutting myself away from the things that come to me unexpectedly? It is funny that I cannot remember feeling those times I have impulsively shared with someone were ever wasted. I have always seemed to come away from them a little refreshed and with a new outlook. Richer, somehow.

Perhaps, like the cruse of oil in the Bible, the time I

give to God is never wasted but is refunded to me in other and better ways.

The phone is ringing now. . . . "Hello? Yes, Anise . . . no, I'm not busy. Just a little ironing. (Now why did I say that!) No, really, it can wait. . . . All right, I promise. See you soon."

I hope she didn't feel my reluctance. Please, please don't let me be irritated. All my good resolves and already I am resisting. Help me to forget myself. She has so much to carry alone. Everyone tells her to leave Gordon. He *is* an alcoholic but she wants to hold on a little longer. She is so sure, with a little more love and God's help, he can find the strength to stop. I wonder how she stands it? This compassion has long ago surpassed her early, physical love for him and yet it is greater even than that first young love that trusted so blindly. Her compassion sees clearly, yet without judgment. He has been unfaithful many times; even the church would condone separation. But she says, "My heart won't let me, nor will God. I can't help it."

No self-pity with Anise. And so many women complain about the things they put up with . . . a leaky faucet in the kitchen, a husband who will not listen, a husband who won't go dancing, children demanding too much time. And they wonder why our sympathy is so thin for them. If they knew Anise . . . if only they knew Anise. . . .

Good or Best?

"What are you two sillies arguing about now?"

"Janie says drinking isn't wrong to do and I say it is wrong. It is wrong, isn't it, Mommy?"

They were both so much in earnest.

"Remember when you girls were helping pick out peaches for me at the market today?"

"Yes. But you haven't answered me, Mommy."

"I'll try to in a minute. Did either of you pick out any rotten peaches?"

"Of course not!" "No."

"Did you choose any with little bruises on them?"

"I found one, but I put it back."

"Why?"

"Because there were better ones."

40

"Was the one you put back all bad?"

"No."

"Every choice we make, in everything, should be made like that. Especially, if we are Christians. People who come to eat in our home expect the nicest food, and people who come to share your life and be your friends expect the best there, too. There are so many things that are not really bad, but they are not the best, either. Anyone can choose between good and bad. That's easy. But it's harder to choose between good and best. Anything you feel you must explain or rationalize probably isn't the best."

"What's 'rationalize'?"

"To try to explain why you do something—usually when you are not sure you should be doing it in the first place."

Janie was studying me quietly. "I know some Christians who drink."

I nodded. "So do I."

"Why don't you all believe the same? Why doesn't your law make you do the same?"

"There cannot be laws for everything, Janie. Christians feel they must live by the Spirit of the law. We feel the better we know Christ, the more we can tell what He would want us to do. Just as you feel about your mother. You can pretty much tell what things she would like you to do and what things might displease her, can't you?"

"Yes, I guess so." She grinned up at me. "She always says, 'When in doubt, don't, because I probably shouldn't be doing it if it bothers me.'"

"That's how we Christians feel. There are a lot of things that are not mentioned in the Bible as being wrong, and yet we don't feel they are the best things for us to do."

"But the Bible says no drunkard can go to heaven, Mommy."

"Yes, but it doesn't say much about drinking without getting drunk." Janie was watching me closely. "My daddy says nothing is wrong if you don't overdo it. Is that the same as Christians feel?"

"No, not exactly. A person can have two drinks and any doctor will show you that that person is not as much in control of himself as he was without them. That's not the best, is it?"

"No. People get silly sometimes. My mother laughs too loud, but she doesn't know it. Daddy's eyes get watery but he walks straight. I don't like the smell. He'll go to heaven, won't he?"

"Janie dear, your daddy's going to heaven depends on more than just whether or not he drinks."

She looked away. "I know. It's how much he loves God, isn't it?"

42

Conformity

"But you should insist that your daughter stay with the group! Really, it's very important, you know, to conform. They need the security of the crowd."

Security. I have seen these pathetic little "belongers" and I do not think they are outstanding examples of poise and self-assurance. They have run so long with the herd that when they stand alone even occasionally, they are positively petrified with fear. They have had the smothering warmth of the pack so long that they shiver without it.

They snarl at a girl who dares to swing her braids and say, "I don't want to. I think it's nasty and I won't do it." They snarl because they know no other way to react. They cannot understand her secret well of sureness. And they huddle together, watching in wonder as she goes the way she wants to go—free as a bird and happy in her decision.

And what of the girl who tossed her head? She is experiencing the wonder of courage. The jewel of jewels, the luxury of doing what she knows is right. She feels the small, very hard core of something very strong and clean inside. Suddenly, her feet have wings and she skips the rest of the way. Her heart is full, her eyes are shining. She broke away for a while and she is not destroyed. She can still walk and pirouette and skip and laugh and run into the wind. She runs home and into my kitchen and the sun comes with her.

"What is it, darling? What wonderful thing happened?"

The skipping ceases, and she smiles at me with a secret in her eyes. "Nothing, Mommy. Nothing much. I just feel so *good!*"

44

Hot Brand and Tender Flesh

What a white, enormous moon there is tonight. With the lights out in the room, I can see the patio flooded with silver. And the moonlight casts the silhouettes of the leaves like delicate black lace across the carpets and here and there against the walls. So peaceful and serene. But inside I churn and ache and cannot give myself to sleep just yet.

We took our girls to see *The Old Man and the Sea* this evening. Our girls wept when the sharks tore into that gallant, vulnerable body of the Great Fish. Our little one said, "Oh, Daddy, I feel so sorry for the Old Man. And for the fish, too."

Then we heard a boy laugh. A boy with the half-changed voice of adolescence, and suddenly the theater was filled with short, sharp guffaws like the frenzied cries of wild coyotes. Anger grabbed me in a hot vise and I could hardly contain myself. Our modern youth—with less respect for valor and the struggle for life, with less recognition of deep emotion than wild animals. Our youth!

When it was over, we rose to take the girls home and then we noticed with surprise that the young people, junior high and high school mostly, were remaining for the second feature. And I thought, "Oh, no. They shouldn't be staying for this!" Something urged me to stay after the family had left. It was Friday night and very few adults were present.

None of the youngsters left. And there was not a sound in that theater during the entire show. There was not a sound during the lewd build-up to an act of adultery. There wasn't a murmur as they soaked up the cynic's view on the utter degradation of man. No one talked through a thoroughly frank dialogue about marital impotence. And there wasn't a snicker as they listened to the account of a husband shooting another man as he climbed out of his wife's bed. Those children absorbed, literally absorbed, every word, every thought, every facial expression and each facet of that disgusting, unnecessary, badly censored film.

I watched their faces as they left the theater, the bald overhead lights hitting the carefully held masks of non-

46

chalance—but showing so pathetically the shock and dismay that lay brooding in their eyes. The light fell on the soft faces of the girls as they avoided the eyes of the boys at their sides. The hoarse young throats cleared themselves for something witty and careful to say.

I wanted to put my arms around them all and say, "I'm sorry!" because anger no longer filled me. A great, sickening shame washed over me and I lowered my face from their gaze.

And we wonder why they do not learn respect and sensitivity? We wonder why, when we place before them "art" like this and rub their fresh, clean, lovely faces in the old stagnant, stinking mud of adult filth and refuse? We wonder why they look at us with disgust when they see how low we can go, how far we fall short, how wretchedly immoral and weak and self-pitying we are? We wonder why they laugh in our faces and sneer at our platitudes when we demand so much of them and they see so much of our failures and coarse emotions in films like this?

They watch our obnoxious passions and spineless mores and they hate us. Of course, they do. What frauds we must seem to them! What white-washed, flabby, insipid, nauseating frauds we must seem in their clear, uncluttered, level look.

Do their parents know what hot iron has been seared into their children's souls tonight? Have these parents even seen the movie? Probably not. Perhaps they were sitting quietly at home, watching TV, playing a harmless game of cards, having cocktails with a few friends—maybe even mentioning with a twentieth-century smile of indulgence that "the children are at the neighborhood theater seeing *The Old Man and the Sea*. Such a stirring picture. We just love our little theater. We feel so safe with the youngsters there."

What was the second feature? "Oh, just some unimportant, offbeat film. You know the type. The kids just sit and eat popcorn through those."

No, they do not just eat popcorn through those. They watch. And they listen. And they record. Like cameras, clearly and permanently. It does not matter whether it is good or bad, decent or obscene, important or offbeat. These lenses are as sensitive and precise as those which come in the German cameras their fathers pay so much money for.

An unimportant film? There is no such thing to a child. Everything is experience and truth, and he will record it as such.

Challenge to Destiny

We read the story of Samuel this evening for devotions. Somehow, that story always fills me with mingled emotions. It is really the story of a mother's plan for her son. The picture of a woman pointing toward the limitless ranges of God's plan for her son—and then of her relinquishing him so that he could go.

This mother of Samuel certainly had nothing but the best in mind for her boy. But she was a practical one, too. She placed him in a position where this goal could be realized. She made his surroundings compatible with the dream and his ability. She saw what he could do, and she made it possible for him to do it.

Of course, we might be inclined to shrink at the

psychological outcome of such highhanded tactics on her part, especially in this brilliant day of "Hands Off the Children" attitude. The boy might have preferred being a shepherd or a merchant instead of a priest and prophet. But, no, on reading it over, we see she made no commitment toward a given profession; she simply gave him to the Lord under the training of a unique and very wise man.

The very fact that Samuel did follow in Eli's steps shows the eloquent way in which the older man had challenged the boy. So the story ends—or rather continues on through history, as God uses Samuel to choose Israel's first king and this king in turn made possible the recognition and establishment of the line of David, and so on through that fabulous history. What if Samuel had not gone to the temple?

I seem almost addicted lately to the habit of wondering if, in the group of boys and girls that pass in and out of our home, there might not be a Man or Woman of Destiny among them. Perhaps one of our own daughters. It thrills me each time I think of it. Yet it fills me with fear, too. Fear that we as parents may fail to keep our children alert to God's call for them. Fear that we may not place them where God can use them. An overwhelming awe in the knowledge of what God can do with one wholly dedicated man or woman. In one short lifetime, He can change the destiny of an entire nation through the willing surrender of one ordinary man with courage and vision.

But Men of Destiny do not run in milling herds. They walk alone. Or no; I do not think they are ever alone, though they feel loneliness at times. Rather, they walk ahead, carrying the tired, struggling masses behind them, up a little higher and a little farther, until those bent figures can see the vistas of freedom too and gain courage for another day of travel.

But where are our Men of Destiny? Men of destruction, men of degradation, men of the streets . . . I must not panic. Of course, there are brave men. But they are hidden away from the crowds, editing papers beyond the smashing fist of the advertising gauntlet, teaching in schools not fettered by small, tiptoeing apple-polishers, raising children with hardly a glance at the book, daring to live up to the best within them, not around them.

Our Men of Destiny. We are not making them any more. The shelves are depleted. Production line items are taking their place—items geared for everything, but fitting nothing. I must not be bitter. Our attempt to free our children from suppression must have originated from a genuine desire to develop a child as an individual. But things have gone sour. Instead of producing individuals, we are stamping out blurred carbon copies at an alarming rate. Nothing new, nothing original—and the world is not buying it.

We have no more Man O' Wars, with hearts bred for the ultimate in achievement . . . only small stunted burros, trudging the narrow trail, tied to the tail of the one in front, eyes on the stones, their burdens chafing and all their lovely, wonderful energy dissipated in kicking out, hurting each other, backing down and braying.

Angel on My Shoulder

The girls are tucked in and the house is sighing softly as the last sounds are sifting quietly into the corners of our lovely room. Sometimes I am sure my house breathes and lives. It has a pulse that I can almost feel at moments like this. It has a way of holding happiness, so tangible that one can feel it when one enters the room.

The firelight flickers like a smile across the chairs and couch and touches the face of my husband as he reads. The breeze that lifts the curtain occasionally is as real as the living I feel around me just now. I hear the gentle murmur of voices through the wall, the last drowsy efforts of weary little girls to resist surrender to sleep.

I get up to close a door that the evening breeze is teasing into bumping and I stop at the sound of their words coming to me. I bend my head to steal just a phrase of their sweet chatter. . . .

"*I'm* never afraid of the dark any more."

"Why?"

"Because there's an angel by my shoulder."

"I don't see it."

"She's there. I can feel her."

"There are no such things any more."

"I have one."

"God keeps us safe." A pause. "Except He seems too big and far away when it's dark. I don't like the dark."

"I know. Mother said I should pray at night when I'm afraid and instead of closing my eyes and hiding under the covers, I should look out and count the stars. It makes me sleepy and I'm not afraid. But when it was cloudy I used to be afraid again. That's when my angel came."

"How did it come?"

"Not it. It's a she."

"How did she come?"

"I asked God to send His Spirit but I didn't want a Spirit because I didn't know what that was exactly. So He sent my angel."

"I don't see her."

"Of course not, silly. But she's there."

"How do you know she's there?"

54

"Because my hands and feet are warm and I'm not afraid any more and I can go right to sleep."

"Can I get an angel, too?"

"I'll pray for one for you. You can talk to her, too."

"What do you say?"

"Just anything. Like when you're sorry for something real bad and you don't exactly want to tell God right away. Then you talk about it to her and it doesn't sound so bad, and you tell God and then you can go to sleep."

"Can my angel come tonight?"

"I don't know. But if she doesn't, you can talk to mine until she does come."

"I'm sleepy now. I'll talk to her tomorrow night."

"All right."

"Goodnight."

Will It Be Too Late?

"Mother, what's an atheist?"

"A person who does not believe in God. He denies that there is a God."

"Oh, poor Rita!"

"Why, dear?"

"Her daddy is an atheist and he says Rita should be, too."

"But I thought she was going to Sunday school with you next Sunday."

"She is but her daddy says he'll give her a dollar if she doesn't believe the kind of stuff they'll teach her there. She loves her daddy so much, Mother."

"Of course, she does. He's a very nice person. I wish he hadn't said that to her, though."

"You aren't even mad at him, Mother."

I looked at the small, disapproving little face. "It makes me very sad, darling. I wish her daddy were not an atheist. It makes me sad for him and it makes me sad for Rita."

"He can't go to heaven if he doesn't believe in God. I told Rita but she says he isn't scared because he says there is no heaven or hell. Rita asked me how I know there's one."

"What did you say?"

"I told her there is, too, because the Bible says so and so does Jesus, and He should know because He came from there."

"Did she believe you?"

"I don't know. I don't think she wants to believe it because she's afraid for her daddy."

I felt a stab of fear myself. I wondered if he knew what is written in the Bible about adults who stand between Him and our children . . . it would be better for us if a stone were hung around our necks and we were drowned in the deepest sea.[1]

"We don't want her to be afraid of God, though. What does Jesus teach instead of fear?"

"He teaches us to love everybody, but I can't help being afraid for Rita, Mother. I like her so much and I'm afraid she'll get sick and die before she believes in God." Her eyes were filling with tears.

"Would she go to hell, Mother?"

[1] Matthew 18:6.

57

"Darling, the lives of children are in God's hands, and His mercy is far greater than ours could ever be. Rita is still a little girl and God understands her troubles."

"But what can I do to help her, Mother?"

"Ask God to take care of her. There are some things we must give to Him because they are too big for us alone. You just stay close to her and love her and explain to her how great God's love is for us all. Don't forget to tell her, too, how God can help her if she will just let Him."

"But I still don't want Rita to die before she believes in God. I can hardly sleep when I think of it."

I took the perplexed little face in my hands. It was so soft and so small and so dear to me. And so worried. "Darling, you must stop worrying about that part of it. That part is in God's hands, and being afraid makes everything worse. God wants Rita to know Him and even if you think you are not helping, remember that nothing we say for Him is ever wasted. You be her friend and be ready to help and leave the rest to God. Some time when she needs Him very much, she'll remember what you told her and it won't be too late."

"Will it be too late for her daddy?"

"I don't know, baby, I don't know. I hope not."

Her Gift

"Mother, how much does a Bible cost?"

"It depends on the kind you want, dear."

"A nice one. White with a zipper and colored pictures. And kind of big."

"Oh, maybe five or six dollars. But you have your black one from Sunday school."

"This isn't for me." She was looking down at her smudgy sheet of paper, at the careful figures she had been making and at the little stacks of coins and scanty bills in front of her on the table. "I have almost six dollars. Would that be enough?"

"Yes, I'm sure it will, but isn't that the money you were saving for your flap-bag? That's all the money you have, isn't it?"

She looked up at me, trusting me, pleading with me to understand with a kind of intensity. "Yes, but I want to buy a Bible for Rita." Her eyes held mine and I know she saw the quick tears that started before I looked away.

I said, "We can get a beautiful Bible for six dollars."

"Does it cost much to have her name put on it?" Her voice was so hopeful.

"No, I don't think so. Would you like that?"

"Yes. In gold in the corner. Gold is pretty on white and then it will be really hers."

"I'm sure she will be very proud of it. And I am very proud of you. I think you are a very nice kind of daughter and I think the angel at your shoulder is smiling now."

She looked up at me and hugged herself. Her eyes were shining with her gift and the warmth from her heart lighted her whole face.

Oh Rita, Rita, will you ever know what this gift cost this child? How long since I have loved so completely and cared so much for someone—or believed in the importance of God to this absolute limit?

First Served, First Love

I wish I had not been so busy today. I wish I hadn't *felt* so busy today. The girls are in bed now and I feel I have cheated them somehow. It seems I denied each request they made, as though each time they tentatively opened a door to me, I quickly closed it. They were not happy when they went to bed. They fussed with each other and the homework still lies here unfinished.

But today was such a bear. It seems everything happened. The hot water heater broke, the washing machine was full of half-washed, soggy clothes, Meg called and wanted to talk for forty-five minutes. Oh, how that girl complains. If it isn't her back, it's her children and if it isn't the children, her husband has done something. Will I ever learn not to ask her how she feels! And then

Kay dropped by for coffee. Coffee, of all things, when I had the laundry to do, the refrig defrosting and the plumber banging around. Then kindergarten was out and the small fry came pounding home. Then there was lunch. And a skinned knee. And a nap and—oh well, why go on. There are just days like this and there will be more. I only wish I didn't have to slight the children. Where's my poise?

And why should I feel guilty? If running a house is so important, why should it bother me when it takes time? All right. I know, I know. Because my family is the most essential thing to me—not housework or getting through with the chores. The house can wait, the family cannot. Having my routine fall apart for one day won't make for a disorganized household. But everyone is affected when the family is shoved aside.

I guess it is just selfishness, wanting my own way, having it undisturbed and untouched by others . . . wanting the satisfaction of having accomplished what I had planned to do, not what needed doing . . . putting lids on everyone else's desire, clamping enthusiasm that isn't parallel with my own, squelching everything that is not neatly pegged "Today's Schedule."

I must change this and soon. This has happened before and rationalization will not solve it. I have sat here many evenings before, muttering to myself handy little phrases that haven't helped a bit.

All right. Tonight I admit it. I was wrong. Never

again. I shall learn to drop anything and say, "OK, I'll help you." Most things take such a short time and the harmony that results is like oil in the machinery. I accede to their small needs and they are content for quite a while. They understand when I am busy. They just want the reassurance that they are still the most important. I don't blame them, either.

This must have been Mother's secret. A secret I always took for granted. I can never remember her saying, "I can't. I'm busy," or "You'll just have to wait. I can't leave this now," or "Just how much do you think I can do at one time?" There was never a time that I can recall.

I do remember Dad bursting into the kitchen through the back door, notebook in hand, coattails flying, and his voice filling the house with, "Melly! Let's go, dear. I'm late," and her "Coming, Louie." Then her quick steps flying down the stairs, her check-out to Dad, "Keys? Notebook? Address? Directions?" and away they would go.

Often I would go upstairs to find the sewing-machine light still on, or a letter half-written, or the iron still warm and a shirt sleeve getting cold and the wrinkles setting. I would pick up the iron and finish the sleeve, or turn off the sewing-machine light—or perhaps I wouldn't. But I always accepted this pattern as perfectly normal procedure.

Until I married, that is, and found unfamiliar phrases

coming out of me like, "Oh, now? I'm right in the middle of this," or "Couldn't it wait? This is the worst time you could pick!"; and even now, I stop and think, "Where did *that* come from?" I suppose the longer I am married, the more my awe for my mother increases.

I try the "Coming, dear" routine but it comes out more like a cross between a whine and a loaded threat. How did you do it, Mother? By determination? No. Heaven knows I have determination.

You just happened to love us so much that you automatically put us first in your routine; that's the secret, isn't it, Mother? Very simple. *Simple!* As much as I adore my family, I do love an organized house and time and again it gets priority. What's that old saying, "First served, first love"? This poses an unpleasant possibility. I must be more careful to put first things first. I just must.

Part of the success will depend on practice and habitual use, I know. Like my devotions each morning; they are such a part of my day. I feel half-groomed without my talk with God each morning. I must put this on my Priority List: Ask God to make me constantly aware of the preciousness of my family. I thank Him each morning, but I must carry this thankfulness through each hour of the day. The more this fills my heart, the more He will help me be open to them. My thankfulness will be so great that it will overflow to them. Each time they speak to me, I shall look full into their eyes and listen.

They will see my love and be reassured. And I shall be filled, too, and more pliable. But I must ask God for this each morning. I cannot do it alone. I've tried.

But it will work. I can hardly wait until tomorrow. I hope it works. . . . But it will! I know it will.

It Worked Today!

"Mommy, where are you?"

"In here, sewing."

"Let's go down to the stream!"

"I can't, dear. I really must finish this pair of curtains."

"Oh, please? It's so beautiful and Mommy, the nasturtiums are all over everywhere and the brook made a tiny little lake and I think there are tadpoles, too. Oh, please come!"

"Darling, I'd love to. You know that. But these curtains have waited so long. Maybe tomorrow. Besides, I have to start dinner soon."

She sighs, resigned at last. "OK, Mommy."

Well, that wasn't as much of a struggle as I thought it would be. Now maybe I can get just two more ruffles

The Wall Between

"What's the matter with you?"

"Mommy's been mad at me lately."

"She's not mad at you, silly. This is just your shaping-up period."

"I know. I've been getting careless about obeying and so I have to be straightened out." (She sounds just like I do when I say it.)

"That's right. And when Mother has to scold you and keep after you, she can't be buddy-buddy. She can't be a mother and a pal at the same time."

"Why not?"

"Because she's so busy making you do what you should do that she can't take time to have fun with you. It's your own fault."

"Did you ever have to be shaped up?"

"Of course, silly. Dozens of times."

"I don't see why."

"Well, good night! Do you want to grow up to be a brat?"

"That's not a nice word."

"I know it, but it describes some people pretty well."

"I'm not a brat."

"No, but you could be if Mother and Daddy don't keep trying to make you behave. And if they can't do it, believe me, no one else will try. You should see some of the kids in my school—as old as me! They're sloppy and they don't follow directions, they lie and cheat— well, you don't want to be like that, do you?"

"No. But I won't be that way."

"You will if you don't start changing. Mother's right. You have been getting away with murder. You don't even pick up your room and I'm always having to finish your chores for you. That isn't right. Each person should be responsible for his own job—without having someone keep after him all the time."

"If I try hard to mind, will Mommy be fun again?"

"Of course, she will. And do you know something? You'll be happier, too."

"I will? That's funny."

"I know it's funny, but it's true. Every time I do something that's wrong, and I keep getting away with it, I just get nastier and meaner all the time. Then when Mother or Daddy catches me on it and I straighten out, I'm fine again. It's funny, but that's the way it is."

"Well, if you say so, I'll try."

"OK. You'll see. It works."

No One Told Me, I Didn't Know

I wish I had not read the paper this morning. Such dumping grounds for human failure. Juvenile delinquents. Divorces, divorces, murders, lawsuits, divorces . . . "My husband resents my working" . . . "My husband is rude to my friends" . . . "My husband brings me extreme and grievous mental suffering." Tears, choked admissions of failure, children with wide eyes and trembling mouths, men with eyes averted, callous and indifferent courtroom employees, but most of all—the hurt, misunderstood, self-pitying woman.

I am a woman. Why do I not feel more sympathy for these women? I know many really have gone through hell before going to court. But what of the others, the majority, like some I know who have just given up? They are the ones who stunt my sympathy and jade my murmurs of condolence. I wish I could write a paper for them all to read. I would simply copy the letter I had from Leah last year, but it might turn them aside for a moment.

How hard it is, though, to dissuade a woman on her way to divorce! She feels if she does not walk out right now, her entire sanity and personality will disintegrate. She feels she simply cannot stand another minute of it. I wonder . . . if she were permitted to glimpse the road ahead, perhaps the road she will be traveling in two years —would that help at all? What if she were to read Leah's letter:

When I filed suit for divorce, I was really being honest when I said I had reached the end of my rope. You know yourself that I believed I was doing the right thing. Nothing looked so good to me as being able to live as I wished with no one countermanding my every action. I was so sick of quarreling and wrangling over absolutely nothing. I thought that being "single" again would be heaven. But it isn't. I'm more unhappy now, more desolate and lonely than I have ever been in my life.

He wasn't perfect and maybe we were not idyllically happy but at least we were together for the big things. He was there when Tod had his operation, I had someone to talk with when I wasn't sure about something; it even helped to worry with someone else about money and the children's discipline. Now I don't even have anyone to tell me if my slip is showing or if my seams are straight!

73

And I miss being with our married friends, too. It's not their fault, but there just isn't a place for me alone, and there certainly aren't enough nice men to go around. This may be a modern world and divorce may be the going thing, but there is no real place for the "single married" woman. It's kind of a dirty trick, to lead us into something like this and then throw us a curve. Why didn't someone tell me it was like this? It's literally jumping from the frying pan into the fire. If only I had found a way to push the pan off the flame. But it's too late now.

And I feel so guilty and defeated. Even the old argument, "I did it for the children," is sagging. The children keep looking at me as though I were something to be pitied, as though I had failed them instead of trying to help them. They just don't grasp the situation. On the surface they pretend to, of course. They repeat the things we've told them, but they sound like little parrots. They don't understand it or really believe it at all.

The children are small now, but what do I do when they are growing up and thinking for themselves? What do I use for an example? *Us?* Hardly.

I remember telling you that I had my pride to think of. Oh, God! What a stupid statement. I don't even know what pride is. I just feel selfish and defeated and aching with the despair. If only I had another chance.

On Trial

I feel as though I must do something about this appalling thing I have just witnessed. Juvenile Court! I wonder how many parents, especially mothers, have ever had a chance or taken the time to sit in on some of these cases. I am sick through and through with thinking of it. I am dumbfounded and unable to grasp the reason for such degradation of young personalities.

At first, I simply refused to believe these young people could be capable of such cynicism and hatred and disrespect. I thought, "Surely this is just a defense mechanism. They must be just frightened inside. They're only a little older than children."

And then one of them looked at me. Full in the face. And the eyes were the eyes of a man, full of stark, stripped, naked knowledge of the human jungle. He had barely enough beard to shave, but his soul was warped hard already and hatred was the acid which formed its shape.

I looked at the pad in my hand, at the swift scribbles I had made. Background data on these youths. Was there a correlation? I read, "broken home," "mother works," "drunken father," "wealthy home," "no car," "not enough to do," "broken home," "parents travel," "mother always tired," "father travels," "not enough spending money," "no one at home," "did it for kicks—we were bored" . . . for kicks? They beat up an old man for kicks? Dear Lord, what makes a boy feel this way? What hatred and resentment must he have against someone to do a thing like this? Let me read his data again: "no one at home."

The judge said, "You live in a very nice neighborhood. Do your parents own their home?"

A level look and a sneer. "Yeah, pop, they own the house."

The judge: "You will address the bench with respect! One more remark like that and you shall be held in contempt."

No indication the boy heard. He inclined his head, nothing more.

"Your mother works. Would it be possible for her to

stay home? I mean, is it necessary that both your parents work?"

The boy shrugged. "I wouldn't know. My mother's a very intelligent woman, you see. She graduated summa cum laude. She hates housework and noisy kids all over. So she works. She can buy a maid. What's the difference?" For the first time, the boy's eyes dropped away from the judge's. His voice dropped, too.

So this was it. I looked around the court. No one here to help him, apparently. Did his mother know? Perhaps she couldn't get off work. But his father—he should be standing here beside him. Such a tall, good-looking boy. Well dressed, too. That cashmere was expensive and he wears it with casual disdain. He's used to nice things. The boys that are with him are nicely dressed, too. They *look* so nice. All but their eyes. Their eyes make me look away.

What would it be like to be young and suddenly realize that you were not very important in your parents' eyes? What would it be like not to be sure if they really loved you with that special, warm, always-for-you way ... the warm, special way I was loved? I cannot imagine not being loved. I cannot imagine my mother shutting herself away from me. I think I would have hated—hated ... yes. Yes, now I feel that hardness, too. I can begin to understand.

I wish I knew where your mother is, now. I would go

77

to her and take her hands and I would make her listen to me. I would beg her to love you and try to make up in these few, almost-gone years, what she has denied you so long.

But I won't go. I will just sit here and hurt for you, and each time I see young shoulders in a cashmere sweater, I will remember.

Wanted: Someone To Follow

It is a gray morning and somehow my heart is gray, too. Heavy and cold and ashamed with what I saw yesterday at court. Even the fire of my anger has gone. My flaming rebellion is gray ashes today and I have no flint to start afresh. How weak and spineless and unused to fighting I must have become. I should do something. There must be something that can awaken a spark of respect and softness in those boys.

They must have dreams of becoming someone. There must be some person they idolize, someone they copy. Boys always have their ideal. It used to be the president. But I don't hear any mother tempt her son with that plum now. Well, naturally not. The presidency of the United States has just become a big pie-throwing board.

No woman wants her boy to be a target for pie-throwers.

How very strange. This change in our attitude toward our leaders, I mean. I wonder when it started? A hundred years ago, even less, these men were expected to stand head and shoulders above the crowd. We just took it for granted that they would lead us onward and upward in spite of our whines and threats and complaints. But we will not respect them any more.

We don't respect anyone any more. That's an awful thing to say . . . but it is true. We don't. We respect mob conformity, group opinion. But that is a Thing, not a person. Well, there must be *someone* these youngsters can idolize. Let me see; push away the TV heroes, the crooners, the rock 'n' roll figures, the athletes and the big-shots and we have about exhausted our outstanding citizens.

Our own daughter brought home an impressive list of preferred vocations the other day that she had copied from school: "actress, singer, politician, baseball player, dancer, guitar player, good guy, big shot, millionaire, and nothing-in-particular." There were a few scattered doctors, lawyers, and news commentators sprinkled here and there, but these professions were contingent on one condition—big money—so they are not as laudable as they might appear on the surface.

Do they really mean this? Or are they hiding, deep inside, a higher drive but one they are afraid to show for fear of ridicule? Where have all the nurses, teachers, mothers, philosophers, missionaries, historians and statesmen gone?

I suppose I know. Naturally, they have no respect for these once highly esteemed positions. Why should they? We, their parents, have no respect for them either. All the children have to do is listen to our adult conversations on modern education, the sad state of our educators' bank books, the tedious, frustrating job of instructing the children we have failed to discipline. Nursing? The hours are terrible and the salaries are not commensurate with the work. Motherhood? Our youngsters don't sense the need of a mother, per se, any more—most of them. They are just as used to baby sitters, housekeepers, nursery-school supervisors and grandmothers. Mother is not the outstanding, irreplaceable person she once was. Besides, she complains so much about being tied down, not having enough help, having too much running around to do and straining to rear her family, that the last thing in the world they would choose would be a leap into a similar predicament.

Statesmen? They do not know what a statesman is. We have a few still, but they are the ones you find cartooned on the editorial page. Though they have always been the favorite meat of the cartoonist, the ridicule has lost its humor now. We believe it.

And so we blame our children for their idols. We

HAND IN HAND

scream at them that they have no respect. They turn
their level gaze on us and they repeat, parrot fashion
with inflections painfully familiar . . . "what's in it for
me? . . . I should stick my neck out . . . not enough
money in it . . . higher wages . . . shorter hours . . . more
vacation . . . too much responsibility . . . too much of a
risk . . . not a sure thing . . . takes too much of my time
. . . what's the point?"

Feeling Is Believing

"Mommy, there isn't really a devil, is there?"

"Yes, there is, dear."

"But Mommy, I've never seen him, have you?"

"No, I have never seen him. But I have felt him."

"But Ann says there is no such thing."

"You tell Ann, darling, that your mother has met Satan, many times. You tell her I know there is one, and that he is just as real as God."

"But Mommy, is he red with a long tail and a fork? I don't believe that!"

"No, I don't think he needs a fork, dear."

"But if you haven't seen him, how do you know?"

"Well, in the first place, the Bible tells us very plainly

that there is a devil. Jesus knew there was. Don't you remember the time the devil took Him into the wilderness to tempt Him?"[1]

"Yes, but maybe that was just His thoughts."

"Satan always works through our thoughts or through other people or through situations. But Jesus still spoke to him as a very real spirit when He said, 'Get thee hence, Satan!' He wasn't talking to Himself."

"But how do *you* know, Mommy?"

I took her into the bedroom and we turned off the light. It was a black night and darkness settled around us quickly. She did not say anything for a moment, and then tentatively, "Mother, why did you turn off the light?" I did not answer. "Mother? Mommy, I know you're here. I'll find you."

I could hear her walking quietly. I remained still, hardly breathing, in the corner. Suddenly I heard her stop, listening and feeling with her whole body for my presence in the room. Then slowly, she came toward me. "You're over here. I can feel you living over here." And she reached out her hand and touched me. Then without another word, she opened the door into the warm light of the hall and her eyes were large and she knew.

"Were you scared when you met him, Mommy?"

[1] Matthew 4:1-11.

84

"Yes, I was frightened. I had never met him before and I didn't know what he would do."

"What did he do, Mommy?"

"He tried to make me hate God, darling. He tried to make me turn away and believe that God had left me."

"Where did he come to you?"

"In the hospital. Everyone else was asleep except me and the attendants. And I felt him by my head. I turned but I couldn't see him, but I was frightened because I knew it was not God. And it was not a person I could touch and see."

"I know. I can feel God sometimes and my angel, too. But it's a warm feeling and I'm not afraid. Did you believe that God had left you?"

"I'm afraid I did doubt and wonder for a while. I'm ashamed of that a little. It seems I argued with Satan all night, until I was too tired to argue any more."

"Why didn't you pray to God to help you, Mommy?"

I looked at her, and smiled. "I did, then, dear. I prayed and told God I couldn't fight any more, that He would have to fight for me."

"Did He, Mommy?"

"Yes. And then it was morning and I wasn't afraid any more. I thought of you children waking up and getting dressed, of you eating your breakfast and of God watching you through the day, and I wasn't afraid any more."

"I love you, Mommy! And I'll never be afraid when I meet the devil. I'll pray like you did and God will fight for me, too, won't He?"

"Yes, darling, He will."

On Purpose or By Chance?

Just as she was leaving, she turned to me and said, "Oh, by the way, I had a very disturbing talk with your daughter last Sunday. She said that you believed God had brought this illness on you. She's mistaken about it, isn't she?"

"Only about part of it. What I said was that I felt God had *given* me this illness, or allowed me to have it." I had to smile a little at the shock on her face.

"But that's an awful thing to say! What will your children think of God? They'll be scared to death of Him!"

"They are not the least bit afraid of Him. In fact, just knowing He is in this with us makes them feel more secure."

"Well, I don't agree with you. I think these things just happen to us. After all, this world is far from perfect with all the disease and everything. Even the Bible says God is no respecter of persons. We take our chances with the rest of the people."

"But we're not just 'the rest of the people,' Helen. The rest of the people really do take their chances, but a Christian turns his life over to God—turns it over completely. If this is true, then there couldn't be an element of 'chance' in what happens to him."

"You honestly think that God could give you a thing like this and still love you? Oh I think you're very much mistaken!"

"Would you prefer to believe that God had gone off and left you to chance? That all the time you thought He was in charge of your life, He wasn't?"

"Well, no, not exactly. But giving you things and allowing you to have them are two different things."

"How are they different in motivation? God is omnipotent; He still has supreme power over what happens to me, whether it is active or permissive on His part. In a case like this, my free will had nothing to do with it. He gave it, or He permitted it—it is still His will for my life."

"Frankly, the thought of going through a catastrophe with God just standing there, letting it happen, simply panics me. I don't know how I'd feel in a situation like yours."

"None of us knows until it happens."

"I don't expect miraculous protection just because I'm a Christian; that seems sort of a sneaky reason for being one. But when I say 'Thy will be done,' I don't expect Him to take me literally! I'm not sure I like this idea of putting my head on a block so willingly."

"I never liked it much, either, so I tried not to think about unpleasant things that happened to others or how I would react in their circumstances. But when it touches you, then you have to think about it. You've got to know, deep down inside, if it comes to you for no reason at all—by chance; or if it happened because of something you did that you knew was wrong; or if it's done because God needs to use it for some purpose. It is very important and I think the only person who can be really sure of the answer is the one affected. And he can only be sure in one way."

"God?"

"Yes. By knowing God so well that nothing He can do would make you doubt His love. By being so sure that you've really trusted Him with your life, that when anything happens, you can think back in an instant and say, 'It happened the way it should have, because I was committed to Him at the time.' That is the only kind of sureness there is, and it is the only thing that finally matters to you . . . the knowledge that God has your life and that every facet of it has meaning and importance to Him."

I Am Afraid

"I'm so afraid I am going to do something that will give Jimmie a psychological reaction to that!" . . . "I'm afraid to break her of that; it might lead to something serious later." . . . "We mustn't be too strict with them. They have to learn by their mistakes." . . . "We mustn't superimpose our wills on theirs. I'm afraid I'll be too dominating!" . . . "We don't take our children to Sunday school; I'm afraid they might react against religion later." . . . "I'm afraid to think of the kind of world our children are growing up in. I'm afraid . . . I'm afraid . . . I'm afraid. . . ."

How very, very sad for us parents. I could just weep for us—and for our children. So bound we are by fear of everything we cannot see with our eyes, of results we cannot measure, of chances we dare not take. We should be strong enough to make decisions for both ourselves and our children, and yet—there is always this fear now.

I wonder if it could be one of the things our youth are fighting against? Our fear. They must sense it. That's funny. They do not need to sense it. They hear it, they watch it, they live with it—this fear of their parents'.

A child is such a free creature, so sure of goodness and all hope for the future. Fear has to be taught them. Caution must be whispered over and over in their ear. And because they cannot believe these whispers, they laugh louder and climb higher and they say, "See, Mom? Here I am and I didn't fall. It's keen up here. You can see way up to the village and even the ocean. Mom! I can see a ship on the ocean. You should come up here!"

But we stay below, the fear crawling over our skin like a live thing. Wanting to go up again, to feel the exhilaration of being high and unafraid and sure.

But it's always the same now. We stand below, holding our hands tight together and letting the fear stalk from our eyes. Our eagles should be off into life. Their wings are strong and quivering with the urge to try. We should be there beside them, taking them higher and higher until we reach the heights where they can see range after range of grandeur, where they can feel the

92

strong winds waiting to lift them aloft, where they can sense the wild winds that could dash them down.

But we grab at them with frightened, clawlike fingers and beg them to stay in the fetid warmth and stillness of the crowded ground, breathing each other's dust and becoming myopic and stupid, flying into petty rages and scratching for grubs like chickens.

We fear and we teach them to fear. We hold to ourselves, and they, too, become apprehensive with uncertainty. They still have the strength of wing and sharpness of eye, and so they scrap harder and flap loudly, they tear and cut and fight, for they were born to flight and they know it and they hate our fear. They want us to fly ahead for them, to show them all the things their hearts have dreamed of. But there is no one to lead them. And so they stay below and become as we are.

We turn on them and we cackle and scold. It hurts to see the wasted youth and beauty. It hurts to see fear destroy . . . our fear. Is there nothing that can free us from it?

Those of us who know what it is to lose this fear, we should be showing others. We who have learned the breathtaking abandon of "letting go and letting God" should be leading the way to those craggy heights. But we are more to blame than the others, for we know what it is to fly. We know the miraculous lift of God's strength. We know what it is to hold still, arms outstretched when we are weary, and let God support us. We know the greatness of His world, we experience the strength He shares with us, we know the vast, full stillness of space that fills and satisfies and gives birth to dreams.

We are to blame for we know that God came not to give us "the spirit of fear; but of power, and of love, and of a sound mind."[1] We know that He can renew our strength; we shall mount up with wings as eagles; we shall run and not be weary; and walk and not faint.[2]

Dear God, help us who know Thee and Thy great sufficiency to lead others to Thee. It is so easy to stay above, removed from the turmoil and confusion and despair below . . . content with You and the plans You share with us. Please, please give us who know the Way the courage and desire to love more these who long to be free from fear, as we now are free.   Amen.

[1] II Timothy 1:7.
[2] Isaiah 40:31.

I Am Looking for God

"Mother, I know it's late but could you talk for just a few minutes?" I stop, my hand on the door. Can she see the eagerness in my heart, the hunger I too feel to be with her just a little longer? She moves the Bible she is reading aside on the bed.

"Mother, when you pray, can you always feel that God is hearing you? I mean, does it ever seem that you're just talking to nothing?"

"Of course. But it doesn't mean that God isn't listening. Usually, I'm thinking about something else, or I'm in a hurry. Or sometimes, the thing I am praying for doesn't mean enough to me. I find the fault is always with me, though."

"I've felt like this for a couple of weeks now and it's a

terrible feeling. Mother, would you think I were just awful if I said I wonder sometimes if there really is a God?"

"No, I wouldn't think you were awful. I should say you were very normal."

"Why?"

"Because everyone goes through a period like this. Every man and woman has to find God for himself. My being a Christian doesn't make you one."

"But it seems the harder I try lately, the farther He seems to go. I just don't get it!"

"Maybe you're working too hard at it. Your soul is like your body, darling. Give it proper nourishment and care —it will grow."

"It seems my body and my mind grow by themselves, but this soul business—I don't know. It seems I have to do all the work and it's not growing at all."

"Maybe you are praying too hard, talking too much. It could be that God is trying to get through to you. Have you ever tried listening?"

She traces a pattern on the sheet with her small, round nail. "Not really, I guess. Oh, I've thought about things I've done wrong, and asked for help not to do them again—things like that. But not really listening for God. No."

"You're old enough to learn how to listen, now. It's the most powerful way God has of working with us. Maybe

He is disturbing you this way so that you will be conscious of what He is trying to tell you."

She looks at me quizzically. "You know—it is sort of like a tuggy feeling. I've felt so restless lately—like something's pushing me or like there's something I need to do and I don't know what it is. Nothing seems to help it."

I feel a sudden electric thrill pass through me. Of course! The tug of God. She is nearly the age I was when I felt it. I smile now, with relief. "I know that feeling, darling. I had it, too. It's like an enormous undertow that no one else notices. It is like being terribly thirsty. It's all the time, isn't it?"

She nods, the wonder coming on her face.

"I always think of it as the Tug of God. And it is nothing you imagine. It is very real. This restlessness is your growing need for God and the pull is His love, in turn, reaching out to draw you to Him. It is the most tremendous pull you will ever feel in your life."

"But what can I do about it, Mother?"

"Just wait, and rest on it. Feel the direction it pulls and go that way. Trust Him. I cannot tell you when you will reach Him, I only know that you will. The only thing that can keep you from God is your fighting to stay away. The fact that you feel Him drawing you shows that you've come close enough already to be within the circle of His power."

"How did you reach Him?"

97

"When I least expected it. I was listening to Handel's *Messiah* and I had never heard the choir and organ so magnificent. And all of a sudden, like a wave building up, I felt God's presence within me. It was so unexpected, yet so unmistakable, that I will never forget it. And suddenly, in just that instant, I knew that He was real, that He was sufficient for anything I should call upon Him for, and that I would never again have to look far or struggle to find Him. When I left the sanctuary, the restlessness was gone, and so was the thirsty feeling I had had so long."

"I wonder how mine will come."

"You may just wake up some morning and the knowledge will be there, lying strong and quiet in your heart. Or it may come to you in a flash as you read a verse in the Bible or hear a sermon or watch a sunrise. It may even be a gradual thing that you won't be able to trace. You will just look back and see that, without knowing it, you are there. But this you must believe, you will reach Him."

I watch the slow, sweet smile I love so much. "I know, Mother. I know I will. I think I've known all along but I just wanted to hear you tell me. Mother, what do people do when they never get rid of this awful feeling? It must be the most terrifying thing in the world . . . never to reach God!"

I look down at her strong, lovely hand . . . the hand that so short a time ago was round and dimpled and always slipping under the protection of mine. Our beautiful daughter will soon be a woman but already her course is set to meet the fabulous current of God's will for her life. How good He is to draw us to Him. Never, in all our feeble striving, could we gain that vast expanse by our own endeavor. Such love draws me to my knees in gratitude.

Too Many People, Too Many Voices

"Moth-er! Make her get out of my room!"

"I'm not hurting you!"

"You're bothering me. Get off my spread! I can't make my bed with you all over the spread. Moth-er!"

Oh, please dear Lord, not another strident, hectic day. I don't think I have the patience to meet it this morning. Help me smile . . . "love is patient and kind" . . . soften my voice—"Now what's all the fussing about?"

"She won't get off my spread and I can't make the bed with her on it."

"She doesn't need the dumb old bedspread yet. She hasn't even changed the top sheet!" She punctuates her remark with a reckless, nasty little face. It always gets results.

"Oh, Mother! Honestly, sometimes I think I'll go off

somewhere else and live! It's just not worth it, being around this pill!"

"I'm not a pill!"

"You are so!"

"I am not!"

"You are. You most certainly are."

"No, I'm not." Tears now—big ones that swell and spill.

"All right, girls, all right. That's enough." A tissue for the small nose, a pat on the tall shoulder. "Get off the spread and come help me fix the lamp shade. You know better than to step all over the spread."

"But, Momma, she wouldn't talk to me!"

I turn to look at my older daughter, remembering her same tearful protest once against being shut out, hoping perhaps my look might remind her gently, too. But no. Not this morning. There is a thin wall of ice between those lovely eyes and mine.

I turn back to the small, huddled shoulders pressed against me. "Well, I'll talk with you. I need some ideas on how to trim the shade."

"But I can always talk to you. I want to talk to *her!* I'm not a baby, am I, Momma? I can talk just as good. She just won't listen." The tears give way to heart-broken sobs.

How can I tell her that her big sister isn't really so big, just now? How can I tell her that this terrible need to be alone has nothing to do with a little sister? The gap just now is too wide, they stand on two different islands. But I must say something. . . .

"You know, if you stop crying, I'll tell you a secret about grownups."

I watch the valiant attempt to stem the tears. Then the little head bobs a tentative "all clear."

"Grownups are funny sometimes. When they have important things to think about, they don't want to be disturbed. You know how you don't like to leave your painting before you're finished? Well, grownups' thoughts are like that sometimes. Maybe Sis has something very important to decide and she needs time alone to do it."

"But I can help her."

"Maybe not. There are some things we have to decide alone."

Her sober little face ponders this a moment. Then she nods suddenly. "OK. I'll go out and help Daddy. I don't think he has anything important to decide now."

I turn back to the bedroom. Shall I go in? She comes to the door instead. Her eyes sullen and resisting. "Oh Mother, you just don't understand."

"Darling, I do understand. I was just making a feeble attempt at truce. She adores you and it hurts when little sisters think they're not wanted."

"So it's all my fault, I suppose!"

"No, it's not all your fault. But you could try to be a

little less violent. Can't you remember how it hurt when you were left out?"

The stubbornness melts around the mouth a bit. "Yes, I guess so. But she's always around, Mother."

"I'll see if I can't help a little more." I smile at her, trying to tease away the ice from her eyes. No luck, and I turn to go.

The back door bangs and more trouble runs through on lithe brown legs. A third voice challenges, "Daddy's waiting for you on the south side! You'd better get going. Mommy, what's she been *doing* all morning? I've been working for hours and Daddy's been waiting for her."

"She" meets this new attack like a tigress at bay. "What have I been doing! I've been trying to get my bed made, that's all! Why don't you help Daddy? You're such an operator."

"Because Daddy wants *you*, that's why!"

"Sure. Anything that needs doing, just call on good old me. No one needs a dray horse when I'm around. I do just fine!" Now she is close to tears but she will wait until her door is closed. Can this be the same girl with whom I talked just last evening? I know it is, and I must be patient.

I turn, half-exasperated, just in time to catch a fleeting glimpse of smug victory on the face beside me. "Now, was that necessary?"

"Well, she shouldn't be so awful. She thinks she's so great lately." The eyes, still teasing, glance toward the door and the voice is louder than it needs to be— "Mommy, what makes big sisters so nasty?"

The bedroom door explodes open. "I heard you, you little stinker! I'll tell you what makes us so 'nasty'! It's horrid *little* sisters like you!" The door slams violently.

I stand here, ragged and tense and wanting to shake them both! My voice rises, "Now that was completely uncalled for. Do you just like to make people angry?"

"Yes. Besides, I'm sick of people this morning."

Yes. Of course. All week, you have been holding your own against other savage little wills at school. In the evenings, you have had to fit in and adjust and gear together—we all have. And by Saturday, we are all tired of people. Even family people. By Saturday we don't feel important to anyone. By Saturday, we feel we have nothing special that anyone wants. By Saturday we are empty.

And then Saturday turns out to be just another day of jobs we don't want to do, of people snapping and tired, of too much noise, too many voices. . . .

"What's in the three baskets, Mother?"
"Three lunches."
"For whom?"
"For you girls."

"Why? Where are we going?"

"We're all tired and cross this morning and I think we need to be alone. I think we need time to be quiet, to think our thoughts, and to talk with God a little."

"Momma, the Bible says to 'Be still and know that I am God.' "

"Yes. Well, that's why each of you is going to choose a spot for lunch and each of you is going to go there alone. Take a book or your knitting or your Jill doll, and don't come back until you feel quiet and sweet inside. Now. Each of you pick a place."

"I've got mine."

"So have I."

"Me too."

"The clearing." She looks around, fearful of challenge. Thank goodness, no argument.

"Second?"

"Under the big pine. By the rock."

"And you?"

"Over at the stream, I guess. By the sand bar. Can I take Tippy with me?" She is the youngest. She needs the comfort of a soft puppy tongue. "Yes, you may take Tippy."

The older girls have gone already, like bright comets leaping down the path. The youngest one lingers, a worn sneaker reluctantly marking a line on the grass. She is too young to be tired of people. She needs people just now, and reassurance and love.

"Would you like to stay and eat with Daddy and me? We might be lonesome."

The face brightens. "Oh yes! I don't need to be alone. I can't hear God very good yet, but I can hear you and Daddy."

The little hands begin to set out her lunch beside ours, assuring her of a place at our table . . . and in our hearts.

Who Is God?

"Momma, who is God?"

"God is a very special person—more wonderful than anyone you have ever known. He is very kind and wise and loves you very, very much."

"What does He look like?"

"No one has ever seen God, dear—not really. He is a spirit."

"What's a spirit?"

"A spirit is—well, it's something you feel. We don't see it with our eyes, but it is real, just the same. There are some things we do not have to see to know about. Like the wind. We can't see the wind, can we?"

She tilts her small, five-year-old face up, squinting against the breeze that ruffles the curls on her shining head. "No, but I can feel it on my face. It tickles my hair. Does God blow on my face?"

"No. We feel God in a different way—we feel Him inside of us in our hearts. We know He's there by the way He makes us feel inside."

Her eyes are very serious, watching me and waiting for something more, something that will make this Wonderful Person real to her.

"God is everything that is good in us. When you are happy and you feel like running, when you love the people around you and want to do things for them, when you mind cheerfully, when you see a rainbow or watch little sunset clouds—then you are feeling God inside you."

"But how can He be in me? I don't feel Him bumping inside me."

"A spirit has no body like you and I have."

"The wind doesn't have a body, but it wiggles the leaves. I can see them move. Can God make things move?"

"Yes, God can do anything."

"But why doesn't He want us to see Him?"

"He said we will see Him when we go to heaven. It is a very special surprise that we have waiting for us there."

"Why does God want to be a spirit?"

"Well, for one thing, He needs to be everywhere. Everyone in the whole world needs Him. If He had a body like ours, He could only be in one place, couldn't He?"

"Yes. Jesus had a body. I have His picture in my Sunday school book. He was God's Son. I could see Him."

"That's right. And now He has gone to be with God but He has sent His Spirit to be inside us, too."

"Does He make me happy?"

"Yes."

"I like to see Him in my book better." A soft little pucker clouds her brow. Suddenly, she looks up and smiles at me. "Jesus loves the little children. I would like to sit on His knee like the children in the picture."

"Of course, you would. And when you're a little older, you will learn to talk with Him, like I do. When we pray, we talk with God and we talk with Jesus. Did you know that?"

"Yes." She looks down at the yellow dandelion in her small, pink fingers. Then, "Do I have to love God?"

"No one *has* to love God. But He loves us very much and He wants us to love Him more than anything in the world."

"But I don't know Him very good."

"Don't worry. As you grow up, you will learn to know Him better and better. Just look at the beautiful world He gave us! He made everything in it—the trees and the flowers, our squirrels, the twinkly stars and the

109

blue sky and the wind. Everything we need or want, God made for us. If you think of God every time you see something beautiful, you will begin to understand Him and you will love Him."

"I think if He made things so purdy that He is very nice. But I would like to see Him. If He has a kind face."

The branch of the big sycamore begins to rustle and shake, and we watch, still and scarcely breathing, as a red, bushy-tailed squirrel makes her nervous, tentative trip down its limb toward the big walnut branch. The rich russet of her coat catches the afternoon sun.

My eyes move to the child beside me, and I know that God is wise in wooing us with beauty. No one is too young to feel Him, no one too insignificant to gain His love. My daughter will know this some day, and now that she has started her trusting way toward Him, my heart will be able to release her more and more into His infinite care and guidance.

The Bridle Chafes
(Everybody's Doing It)

"Why are you mad at Mommy?"

"I'm not really mad at Mother. I'm just—oh! you wouldn't understand!"

"Yes I would. Please tell me. I will understand."

"Well, I want to join the club and Mother says I can't. And everyone else is going to."

"Why won't she let you?"

"Because she doesn't think it's a good idea. She doesn't think cliques are particularly nice." (How well she imitates the tone of my voice!)

"Well, I think she's mean! I don't think that's very nice!"

"It isn't Mother's fault."

"She's just being mean."

"She is *not* being mean! She's doing what she feels is right!"

"Well, don't get mad at me. I'm on your side."

"Oh, you just don't understand! Forget it!"

Silence. A kind of hurt silence and I can picture the troubled, bewildered look as her offering of friendship is rejected. Then she tries again.

"But Sis?"

"What?"

"Is there anything the matter with clubs?"

"Oh, not exactly. The principal doesn't approve. And sometimes they have parties that—well, that Mother doesn't like. I guess that's the reason."

"What kind of parties?"

"You wouldn't understand."

"Yes I would too. I bet they're parties with boys, aren't they?"

"Yes. Now why don't you leave me alone?"

"Because I want to talk with you. Why do the other mothers let their girls join?"

"I really don't know. I didn't ask!"

"Sis, if you were a mother, would you let your daughter join?"

A long silence. "No. No, I don't think so."

"Well, gee! Why get mad at Mommy, then?"

"I told you—I'm not mad at Mother!"

"You were, too!"

"I was not. I'm just mad at—at everything! So just go away and leave me alone!"

"All right, I will. But I don't understand why you get so mad. I don't understand growing-up sisters. They're all mixed up." She leaves now, completely dejected and alone. She tried so hard to build a little bridge with her love and ten-year-old compassion. And it was not long enough. It always hurts a little to be left behind. It hurts when love is not enough.

My New Friend, Alice

What a lesson I have learned from you today, my little six-year-old. As I sit here, watching your shiny, blonde, pony-tailed head bent close to the curly, black one beside you, my heart, at first walking the precarious rope of smugness, now bows in humility before your pure, uncorrupted eyes of childhood.

It was yesterday that you asked me if your friend could play, and I asked, "What friend, dear?"

"My new friend, Alice."

"Oh? Is she fun to be with?"

"Oh yes! She laughs all the time and she has all her second teeth already. She wears ribbons in her hair and she likes to jump rope."

"I think that would be very nice. Is she new at day

camp?" You were quiet for just a hesitating moment. Then, a little puzzled, you said, "Yes. She's new. She seemed kind of scared at first. That's why I made friends with her."

"Oh. What does she look like?"

"She has brown eyes and black hair and she laughs down here (you pointed to your soft pink throat). She can run faster than I can but I can win her playing handball. And her skin is so smooth, Momma."

Her mother called me last night. She said, "My daughter tells me that she has been invited to play with your daughter tomorrow. I wanted to be sure it met with your approval."

I did not think much about it, because you Little Women do make plans quite independently at times. I did not even think much about the extra warmth in her voice at my reassurance that it was fine with me.

I did not really understand until you brought Alice home today, proud and laughing, and I looked at the beauty of you two together as you stood before me— two little girls with brown eyes shining and hands held between you.

And you were right, my baby. Her skin is beautiful . . . like deep, rich mahogany against the pale glow of your own. . . .

The Vigil

Her face is so flushed, and her hand here in mine, so
hot, so very hot—oven-dry and seemingly weightless.
Dear Lord, she is so sick and I am so afraid. I try to pray,
yet the words are separate from my heart; the phrases
are familiar but they have no roots deep in my soul where
the ache lies, silent and ready to spring. I am afraid to
look there, or to listen. My soul whispers, "Surrender,
release her," and my mother heart cries in anguish "No!
No, no, no. . . ." How can I lift her up to You of my
own will? You could not need her as I do.

I am so weary and I cannot pray, I cannot pray. Nor
can I hear You. My soul holds its hands over its ears and
I bend away from the possible.

Her breathing is labor, every small, beautiful muscle

quiet while her body throws itself against this enemy. The waiting face of a child, even in pain, so trusting. There is no wild-eyed fear, no frantic clawing for help. Just an occasional look, a quiet, soft search for reassurance. I am here, darling, I am here.

My soul and heart are reaching for her, like the breath of warmth across a cold room. My living is Will so tangible that her small sturdy feet could walk upon it just now. All my thoughts are cables supporting this bridge for her. I hardly dare breathe for fear it will sag the short instant she may need it. My eyes burn, yet cannot leave her face. My back aches, my arm, yet even this pain is a cable for my love.

I hope someone is praying for her, and for me. I cannot do it just now. Somehow I cannot find the courage to seek Your face and know the truth. I do not want to know if she will be mine or Yours . . . not just now, please. Just stay close beside us, Your hand on my shoulder and Your love upon her and around her. I just ask the knowledge of Your presence and the assurance that You are here, and that I will be strong enough. . . .

The Light Touch

"Hi! Come on in!"

"Oh, what a fabulous shade of lipstick!"

"Isn't it the most? I just got it today."

The breezy slam of the front door, the shy but polite "Hello" to me, and they are off for another session of giggles and exchanged advices, whispered conferences and shrieks of "Oh no! You're kidding!"

This wonderful, kaleidoscopic age of the pre-teen. I walk on tiptoe, ready to laugh one minute, protest the next—firm yet pliable, understanding but not weak. And always, always the light touch and the hidden place for my fear or concern.

"Mother, do you mind if we use the kitchen? We're simply dying for some fudge."

"No, not at all. I just need one sink for the strawberries. Want some?"

"Mmmm, yes. Aren't they fabulous! For jam?"

"No—strawberry shortcake. I hope."

The new, sophisticated brush on the cheek—to save lipstick. "You're a doll, Mother."

"Thank you. You're pretty fair yourself."

The laughing shrug. "My mother—a master at understatement. Isn't she the most?"

"The most . . . fabulous . . . the end." What were the terms we used at this age—"out of this world . . . terrific"? That's funny. I can't remember. I do remember Mother saying, "Oh, I'll be so glad when you find another phrase!" That didn't seem so long ago, yet here I am, listening to my own daughter and feeling the same way. The human comedy, the pattern the same.

"Ooh, I bet I gain three pounds on this. Say, did you see Pat today? With that new boy?"

"Yes. Wasn't she just gone?"

"I wouldn't be caught dead with him."

Already they have forgotten I am here. Lately, she has allowed me this rare privilege—this opportunity of being the unseen guest. As long as I do not intrude on the conversation, or offer my opinion. As long as I am the unheard member, I am tolerated and offered a place within their circle. And I am so careful, so cautious with this casual gift—though sometimes I almost forget and have to bite my lip and think, "Pretend you are not here. You mustn't speak. You mustn't say it now—wait until later. There will be a time. . . ."

"And you know the type he is."

"That's for sure. The sugar's up there on the third shelf. Did you know she's going to the senior party with him? It's just going to be a big make-out."

Oh, that phrase! Well, ours sounded just as bad, I suppose—necking, pitching woo.

"That's all she goes to Friday night shows for, you know."

"I know. It makes you sick."

"Wait. That's too much chocolate. Mother, where's the vanilla?"

"It should be right there, behind the spices."

"Oh, I see it. Oh help!" A crash—complete chaos as the spice rack falls. Then dead silence. Then shrieks of laughter. It's not really funny, but seeing them sitting there, in the middle of the débris, giggling and laughing till tears roll down their cheeks, makes me laugh suddenly too and then everything looks ridiculous. The two of them, hilarious and unperturbed at the mess of cinnamon and cloves, nutmeg and marjoram.

"I know!" More giggles. "Let's make the fudge here on the floor!" And they are off again, in helpless gales, struggling and gasping for breath.

But they will clean it up, not right away and probably not perfectly. I may find some cloves under the sink tomorrow and crunch a bit of glass when I cross the floor, but they will make a stab at it.

And I feel better already, after my laugh. What would I do without the girls in the house? How stagnant and colorless the days would be. How unimportant my work around the house, how pointless the polished furniture or vase of flowers. I love the tennis racket against the bedroom couch and the sweater draped across the bed, where it didn't quite make it to the drawer. The books with tattered covers and purses stuffed to bulging. The folded notes, dog-eared and furtively jammed in pockets, the bobby-pins on the table and the apple core—carefully placed on the paper napkin, but still on the coffee table.

All these mute calling cards that tell me my girls are home. That they still live here and that for a while yet, they will be coming and going through these doors, sleeping in their beds and brushing their sweet kisses against my face. I treasure every hour, every word, every carefree action they share with me.

And I am grateful, so very grateful. If only I could remember everything. These laughing afternoons, the special sound of her own giggle. The way her hands move among the bits of broken bottles, the way she throws her head back, the line of her cheek and the special curve of her mouth.

Memory is unpredictable, though. Sometimes these things come back, like colored etchings, on an unsuspected day. And other times, they are obliterated, like footprints on the sand after the tide has washed in.